THORBURN'S ATLAS OF EUROPEAN BIRDS

THORBURN'S ATLAS OF EUROPEAN BIRDS

Original Watercolor Illustrations
by
ARCHIBALD THORBURN

Selected and Edited
by
GEORGES THALMANN

BLANDFORD

A BLANDFORD BOOK
First published in the UK 1994 by Blandford
A Cassell Imprint
Cassell plc, Villiers House
41-47 Strand, London WC2N 5JE

Distributed in the United States by Sterling Publishing Co., Inc.
387 Park Avenue South, New York, NY 10016-8810

Distributed in Australia by Capricorn Link (Australia) Pty Ltd
2/13 Carrington Road, Castle Hill, NSW 2154

A catalogue data entry for this title is available from the
British Library

ISBN 0-7137-2446-3

Printed and bound in Italy

INTRODUCTION

After thorough and systematic selection from the wide variety of common names given to the same bird, this atlas uses that most commonly accepted and used by ornithologists in French, English, German, Italian and Spanish.

The scientific names – the Latin names – are based upon the principles of the Swedish naturalist Carl von Linné (Linnaeus) in his *Systema Naturae* of 1735. They correspond to those cited in the reference work of Professor K.H. Woous (see Bibliography) with the usual designations of Genus, species and sub-species (race).

If male and female present characteristics which are barely visible in nature, they are differentiated by the symbol 0. Size differences are indicated by the sign $>$. For example, the abbreviation $\male < \female$ shows that the male is smaller than the female.

Breeding and overwintering zones are represented on the maps, or by the letters indicating countries where the bird has been observed. The coloured zone on each map indicates the breeding area of the same species or race.

A bird's wintering distribution outside of the geographical region occupied in the mating season is shown below or inside a line of arrows. In certain birds, this area coincides with the breeding area.

Each species or sub-species adapts to its own natural habitat, where lifestyle and plumage are varied to suit the environment. These adaptations can present important differences, or merely slight nuances. Such differences are particularly evident in the mating season and provide an important recognition point. Thus, if the change is marked, different summer, autumn and winter plumages are indicated by the letters S, A and W.

If neither symbol $\male$ nor $\female$ is specified after the Latin name, it generally represents the male.

[Only the Great Auk carries the sign + as indication of the sad fact that this species is extinct.]

Finally, names followed by the letter R designate birds rarely seen in Europe.

ABBREVIATIONS	*ABRÉVIATIONS*	ABKÜRZUNGEN	*ABBREVIAZIONI*	ABREVIATURAS
o	Adult	*Adulte*	Erwachsen	*Adulto*	Adulto
♂	Male	*Mâle*	Männchen	*Maschio*	Macho
♀	Female	*Femelle*	Weibchen	*Femmina*	Hembra
(J)	Juvenile	*Jeune*	Jung	*Giovane*	Joven
(L)	Scientific name	*Nom scientifique*	Wissenschaftlicher Name	*Nome scientifico*	Nombre científico
(A)	Autumn	*Automne*	Herbst	*Autunno*	Otoño
(S)	Summer	*Été*	Sommer	*Estate*	Verano
(W)	Winter	*Hiver*	Winter	*Inverno*	Invierno
(R)	Rare	*Rare*	Selten	*Raro*	Raro
†	Extinct	*Éteint*	Ausgestorben	*Estinto*	Extinguido
<	Smaller than	*Plus petit que*	Kleiner als	*Più piccolo della*	Más pequeño que

MAPS	*CARTES*	KARTEN	*CARTINE*	MAPAS

| Coloured area: breeding range (summer). | *Zone en couleur: aire de nidification (été).* | Farbige Zone: Brutgebiet (Sommer). | *Zona a colori: area di nidificazione (estate).* | Zona en color: área de cría (verano). |
| Winter range: area below or within the broken line. | *Aire d'hivernage: zone au-dessous ou à l'intérieur de la ligne de tirets.* | Winterquartier: Gebiet unterhalb oder innerhalb der Strichlinie. | *Area di svernamento: area al di sotto o all'interno della linea tratteggiata.* | Área de invernada: zona por debajo o dentro de la línea punteada. |

The following symbols designate the countries where certain species of birds have been observed, without breeding range map.

Les symboles ci-après désignent les pays où ont été observés certaines espèces d'oiseaux, sans carte d'aire de nidification.

Die folgenden Symbole bezeichnen die Länder, in denen gewisse Vogelarten beobachtet wurden (ohne Brutgebietskarte).

I seguenti simboli indicano i paesi dove sono state osservate certe specie di uccelli, senza cartina di area di nidificazione.

Los símbolos siguientes indican los países donde han podido observarse ciertas especies de aves sin mapa de área de cría.

A	Austria	*Autriche*	Österreich	*Austria*	Austria
B	Belgium	*Belgique*	Belgien	*Belgio*	Bélgica
CH	Switzerland	*Suisse*	Schweiz	*Svizzera*	Suiza
CS	Czechoslovakia	*Tchécoslovaquie*	Tschechoslowakei	*Cecoslovacchia*	Checoslovaquia
D	Germany	*Allemagne*	Deutschland	*Germania*	Alemania
DK	Denmark	*Danemark*	Dänemark	*Danimarca*	Dinamarca
E	Spain	*Espagne*	Spanien	*Spagna*	España
F	France	*France*	Frankreich	*Francia*	Francia
GB	Great Britain	*Grande-Bretagne*	Grossbritannien	*Gran Bretagna*	Gran Bretaña
H	Hungary	*Hongrie*	Ungarn	*Ungheria*	Hungría
I	Italy	*Italie*	Italien	*Italia*	Italia
IRL	Ireland	*Irlande*	Irland	*Irlanda*	Irlanda
IS	Iceland	*Islande*	Island	*Islanda*	Islandia
M	Malta	*Malte*	Malta	*Malta*	Malta
N	Norway	*Norvège*	Norwegen	*Norvegia*	Noruega
NL	Holland	*Pays-Bas*	Niederlande	*Paesi Bassi*	Países Bajos
P	Portugal	*Portugal*	Portugal	*Portogallo*	Portugal
S	Sweden	*Suède*	Schweden	*Svezia*	Suecia
SF	Finland	*Finlande*	Finnland	*Finlandia*	Finlandia
YU	Yugoslavia	*Yougoslavie*	Jugoslawien	*Iugoslavia*	Yugoslavia

1

Turdus viscivorus
Mistle Thrush
Grive draine
Misteldrossel
Tordela
Zorzal Charlo

4

Turdus iliacus
Redwing
Grive mauvis
Rotdrossel
Tordo sassello
Zorzal Alirrojo

2

Turdus pilaris
Fieldfare
Grive litorne
Wacholderdrossel
Cesena
Zorzal Real

5

Turdus philomelos
Song Thrush
Grive musicienne
Singdrossel
Tordo bottaccio
Zorzal Común

3

Turdus ruficollis atrogularis
Black-throated Thrush
Grive à gorge noire
Schwarzkehldrossel
Tordo golanera
Zorzal Papinegro

F, GB, I, N

♀ ♂

Mistle-Thrush

Black-Throated Thrush
♂ & ♀.

Song-Thrush

Fieldfare

Redwing

Archibald Thorburn
1913

2

(L)
ENGLISH
FRANÇAIS
DEUTSCH
ITALIANO
ESPAÑOL

1

F, GB, I, N

Turdus sibiricus
  (Zoothera sibirica)
Siberian Thrush
Merle sibérien
Sibirische Drossel
Tordo siberiano
Zorzal Siberiano

4

Turdus torquatus
Ring Ouzel
Merle à plastron
Ringdrossel (Ringamsel)
Merlo dal collare
Mirlo Capiblanco

2

E, F, GB, I, N

Zoothera dauma
White's Thrush
Grive dorée
Erddrossel
Tordo dorato
Zorzal Dorado

5

Monticola saxatilis
Rock Thrush
Merle de roche
Steinrötel
Codirossone
Roquero Rojo

3

F, GB, I, N

Turdus naumanni eunomus
Dusky Thrush
Grive à ailes rousses
Rostflügeldrossel
Cesena fosca
Zorzal Eunomo

6

Turdus merula
Blackbird
Merle noir
Amsel
Merlo
Mirlo Común
♂ ♀

Pl. 2

Siberian Thrush   White's Thrush   Dusky Thrush

Ring-Ouzel   Blackbird   Rock Thrush

3

(L)
ENGLISH
FRANÇAIS
DEUTSCH
ITALIANO
ESPAÑOL

1

GB, H, I

Oenanthe pleschanka
Pied Wheatear
Traquet pie
Nonnensteinschmätzer
Monachella dorsonero
Collalba Pía

5

GB, I, S,SF

Oenanthe deserti
Desert Wheatear
Traquet du désert
Wüstensteinschmätzer
Monachella del deserto
Collalba Desértica

2

F, GB, M

Oenanthe isabellina
Isabelline Wheatear
Traquet isabelle
Isabellsteinschmätzer
Culbianco isabellino
Collalba Isabel

6

Oenanthe leucura
Black Wheatear
Traquet rieur
Trauersteinschmätzer
Monachella nera
Collalba Negra

3

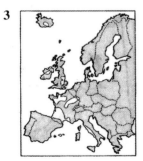

Oenanthe oenanthe
Wheatear
Traquet motteux
Steinschmätzer
Culbianco
Collalba Gris

♂ ♀

7

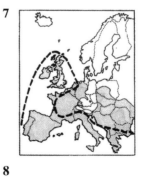

Saxicola torquata hibernans
Stonechat
Traquet pâtre
Schwarzkehlchen
Saltimpalo
Tarabilla Común

4a

Oenanthe hispanica melanoleuca
Black-eared Wheatear (black-
    throated form)
*Traquet oreillard (forme dite
    stapazin ou à gorge noire)*
Mittelmeersteinschmätzer
    (schwarzkehlige Phase)
Monachella (forma dalla gola nera)
Collalba Rubia (forma gorginegra)

(S)

8

GB

Saxicola torquata rubicola
Eastern Stonechat
Traquet pâtre oriental
Ostschwarzkehlchen
Saltimpalo orientale
Tarabilla Oriental

(R)

4b

Oenanthe hispanica hispanica
Black-eared Wheatear (white-
    throated form)
*Traquet oreillard
    (forme "oreillard")*
Mittelmeersteinschmätzer (weiss-
    kehlige Phase)
*Monachella (forma dalla gola chia-
ra)*
Collalba Rubia (forma gorgiblanca)

(S)

Pl. 3.

A. Thorburn
1913

Wheatear ♂ & ♀.
Desert-Wheatear
Eastern Stonechat

Pied Wheatear
Isabelline Wheatear
Black-throated & Black-eared Wheatears
Black Wheatear   Stonechat

4

1

Phoenicurus phoenicurus
Redstart
Rougequeue à front blanc
Gartenrotschwanz (Gartenrötel)
Codirosso
Colirrojo Real

2

Erithacus rubecula
Robin (Redbreast)
Rougegorge
Rotkehlchen
Pettirosso
Petirrojo

3

Phoenicurus ochruros
Black Redstart
Rougequeue noir
Hausrotschwanz (Hausrötel)
Codirosso spazzacamino
Colirrojo Tizón

4

Saxicola rubetra
Whinchat
Traquet tarier
Braunkehlchen
Stiaccino
Tarabilla Norteña

5

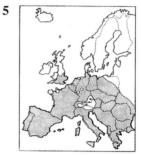

Luscinia megarhynchos
Nightingale
Rossignol philomèle
Nachtigall
Usignolo
Ruiseñor Común

6a

Luscinia svecica cyanecula
White-spotted Bluethroat
Gorgebleue à miroir blanc
Weisssterniges Blaukehlchen
Pettazzurro occidentale
Pechiazul Medalla Blanca

(S)

6b

Luscinia svecica svecica
Red-spotted Bluethroat (Arctic Bluethroat)
Gorgebleue à miroir roux
Rotsterniges Blaukehlchen
Pettazzurro orientale
Pechiazul Medalla Roja

DK, N, S, SF (S)

Pl.4

Redstart   Redbreast

Black Redstart   Whinchat   Nightingale

White-spotted Bluethroat   Arctic Bluethroat

5

(L)
ENGLISH
FRANÇAIS
DEUTSCH
ITALIANO
ESPAÑOL

1

Sylvia communis
Whitethroat
Fauvette grisette
Dorngrasmücke
Sterpazzola
Curruca Zarcera

2

Sylvia curruca
Lesser Whitethroat
Fauvette babillarde
Klappergrasmücke
Bigiarella
Curruca Zarcerilla

3

Sylvia atricapilla
Blackcap
Fauvette à tête noire
Mönchsgrasmücke
Capinera
Curruca Capirotada
♀ ♂

4

Sylvia hortensis
Orphean Warbler
Fauvette orphée
Orpheusgrasmücke
Bigia grossa
Curruca Mirlona

5

Sylvia nisoria
Barred Warbler
Fauvette épervière
Sperbergrasmücke
Bigia padovana
Curruca Gavilana

6

Sylvia melanocephala
Sardinian Warbler
Fauvette mélanocéphale
Samtkopfgrasmücke
Occhiocotto
Curruca Cabecinegra

7

Luscinia luscinia
Thrush Nightingale
Rossignol progné
Sprosser
Usignolo maggiore
Ruiseñor Ruso

8

Sylvia borin
Garden Warbler
Fauvette des jardins
Gartengrasmücke
Beccafico
Curruca Mosquitera

Pl. 5.

Whitethroat

Lesser Whitethroat

Blackcap ♂♀   Barred Warbler   Orphean Warbler

Thrush-Nightingale   Sardinian Warbler   Garden-Warbler

2/3

6

1

A, CH, D, DK, F,
GB, I, IRL, N, NL

Phylloscopus inornatus
Yellow-browed Warbler
Pouillot à grands sourcils
Gelbbrauenlaubsänger
Luì forestiero
Mosquitero Bilistado

5

Phylloscopus trochilus
Willow Warbler (Willow-Wren)
Pouillot fitis
Fitis
Luì grosso
Mosquitero Musical

2

Sylvia cantillans
Subalpine Warbler
Fauvette passerinette
Weissbartgrasmücke
Sterpazzolina
Curruca Carrasqueña

6

Phylloscopus trochiloides
Greenish Warbler (Greenish
   Willow-Warbler)
Pouillot verdâtre
Grünlaubsänger
Luì verdastro
Mosquitero Troquiloide

3

B, DK, F, GB, H,
N, NL, S, SF,YU

Phylloscopus proregulus
Pallas' Warbler (Pallas Willow-
   Warbler)
Pouillot de Pallas
Goldhähnchenlaubsänger
Luì del Pallas
Mosquitero de Pallas

7

Phylloscopus sibilatrix
Wood Warbler (Wood-Wren)
Pouillot siffleur
Waldlaubsänger
Luì verde
Mosquitero Silbador

4

Sylvia undata
Dartford Warbler
Fauvette pitchou
Provencegrasmücke
Magnanina
Curruca Rabilarga

8

Phylloscopus collybita
Chiffchaff
Pouillot véloce
Zilpzalp
Luì piccolo
Mosquitero Común

Pl. 6.

Subalpine Warbler.

Dartford Warbler.　　Willow-Wren.

Wood-Wren

Yellow-browed Warbler

Pallas's Willow-Warbler

Greenish Willow-Warbler

Chiffchaff　　2/3

7

1

Hippolais polyglotta
Melodious Warbler
Hypolaïs polyglotte
Orpheusspötter
Canapino
Zarcero Común

4

E, F, GB, NL, S

Phylloscopus schwarzi
Radde's Warbler (Radde's Bush-
   Warbler)
Pouillot de Schwarz
Bartlaubsänger
Luì di Schwarz
Mosquitero de Schwarz

2

Hippolais icterina
Icterine Warbler
Hypolaïs ictérine
Gelbspötter
Canapino maggiore
Zarcero Icterino

5

Acrocephalus palustris
Marsh Warbler
Rousserolle verderolle
Sumpfrohrsänger
Cannaiola verdognola
Carricero Políglota

3

Cercotrichas galactotes
Rufous Bushchat (Rufous Warbler)
Agrobate roux
Heckensänger
Usignolo d'Africa
Alzacola

6

Acrocephalus scirpaceus
Reed Warbler
Rousserolle effarvatte
Teichrohrsänger
Cannaiola
Carricero Común

Melodious Warbler   Icterine Warbler
Rufous Warbler   Radde's Bush-Warbler

8

(L)
ENGLISH
FRANÇAIS
DEUTSCH
ITALIANO
ESPAÑOL

1

Acrocephalus schoenobaenus
Sedge Warbler
Phragmite des joncs
Schilfrohrsänger
Forapaglie
Carricerín Común

2

Locustella luscinioides
Savi's Warbler
Locustelle luscinioïde
Rohrschwirl
Salciaiola
Buscarla Unicolor

3

Cettia cetti
Cetti's Warbler
Bouscarle de Cetti
Seidensänger
Usignolo di fiume
Ruiseñor Bastardo

4

Acrocephalus arundinaceus
Great Reed Warbler
Rousserolle turdoïde
Drosselrohrsänger
Cannareccione
Carricero Torda

5

Acrocephalus paludicola
Aquatic Warbler
Phragmite aquatique
Seggenrohrsänger
Pagliarolo
Carricerín Cejudo

6

Locustella naevia
Grasshopper Warbler
Locustelle tachetée
Feldschwirl
Forapaglie macchiettato
Buscarla Pintoja

Pl. 8.

Sedge-Warbler   Savi's Warbler
Cetti's Warbler   Great Reed-Warbler   Aquatic Warbler
            Grasshopper-Warbler

9

(L)
ENGLISH
FRANÇAIS
DEUTSCH
ITALIANO
ESPAÑOL

1

Regulus regulus
Goldcrest
Roitelet huppé
Wintergoldhähnchen
Regolo
Reyezuelo Sencillo

5

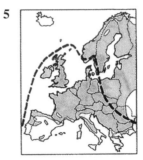

Prunella modularis
Dunnock (Hedge-Sparrow)
Accenteur mouchet
Heckenbraunelle
Passera scopaiola
Acentor Común

2

Regulus ignicapillus
Firecrest
Roitelet triple bandeau
Sommergoldhähnchen
Fiorrancino
Reyezuelo Listado

6

Prunella collaris
Alpine Accentor
Accenteur alpin
Alpenbraunelle
Sordone
Acentor Alpino

3

Sitta europaea
Nuthatch
Sittelle torchepot
Kleiber
Picchio muratore
Trepador Azul

7

Cinclus cinclus
Dipper
Cincle plongeur
Wasseramsel
Merlo acquaiolo
Mirlo Acuático

4

Troglodytes troglodytes
Wren
Troglodyte
Zaunkönig
Scricciolo
Chochín

Pl. 9

Goldcrest
Firecrest
Wren

Nuthatch
Hedge-Sparrow

Archibald Thorburn
1913

10

(L)
ENGLISH
FRANÇAIS
DEUTSCH
ITALIANO
ESPAÑOL

1

Aegithalos caudatus
Long-tailed Tit (Titmouse)
Mésange à longue queue
Schwanzmeise
Codibugnolo
Mito

5

Parus cristatus
Crested Tit
Mésange huppée
Haubenmeise
Cincia dal ciuffo
Herrerillo Capuchino

2

Parus palustris
Marsh Tit
Mésange nonnette
Sumpfmeise
Cincia bigia
Carbonero Palustre

6

Parus caeruleus
Blue Tit
Mésange bleue
Blaumeise
Cinciarella
Herrerillo Común

3

Panurus biarmicus
Bearded Tit
Mésange à moustaches
Bartmeise
Basettino
Bigotudo
♀ ♂ ♂

7

Parus ater
Coal Tit
Mésange noire
Tannenmeise
Cincia mora
Carbonero Garrapinos

4

Parus major
Great Tit
Mésange charbonnière
Kohlmeise
Cinciallegra
Carbonero Común

Pl. 10.

Marsh-Titmouse.   Long-tailed Titmouse.   Bearded Titmouse.
δ & ♀.
Great Titmouse.

Coal-Titmouse.   Crested Titmouse.   Blue Titmouse.

2/3

11

(L)
ENGLISH
FRANÇAIS
DEUTSCH
ITALIANO
ESPAÑOL

1

Tichodroma muraria
Wallcreeper
Tichodrome échelette
Mauerläufer
Picchio muraiolo
Treparriscos

(W) (S)

2

Certhia familiaris
Treecreeper
Grimpereau des bois
Waldbaumläufer
Rampichino alpestre
Agateador Norteño

3

B, F, GB

Motacilla alba yarrellii
Pied Wagtail
Bergeronnette de Yarrell
Trauerbachstelze
Ballerina nera
Lavandera Blanca Enlutada

4

Motacilla flava flava
Blue-headed Wagtail
Bergeronnette printanière
Schafstelze
Cutrettola
Lavandera Boyera

5

Motacilla alba alba
White Wagtail
Bergeronnette grise
Bachstelze
Ballerina bianca
Lavandera Blanca Común

6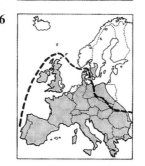

Motacilla cinerea
Grey Wagtail
Bergeronnette des ruisseaux
Gebirgstelze (Bergstelze)
Ballerina gialla
Lavandera Cascadeña

7

Motacilla flava thunbergi
Grey-headed Wagtail (Grey-headed Yellow Wagtail)
Bergeronnette printanière nordique
Nordische Schafstelze
Cutrettola caposcuro
Lavandera Boyera Escandinava

8

GB

Motacilla flava flavissima
Yellow Wagtail
Bergeronnette flavéole
Englische Schafstelze
Cutrettola inglese
Lavandera Boyera Inglesa

Pl. 11.

Wall-Creeper (summer & winter).
Pied Wagtail.
White Wagtail.
Grey-headed Yellow Wagtail.

Tree-Creeper.
Blue-headed Wagtail.
Grey Wagtail.
Yellow Wagtail.

12

(L)
ENGLISH
FRANÇAIS
DEUTSCH
ITALIANO
ESPAÑOL

1

Anthus spinoletta petrosus
Rock Pipit
Pipit maritime
Strandpieper
Spioncello marino
Bisbita Ribereño Costero

5

Anthus cervinus
Red-throated Pipit
Pipit à gorge rousse
Rotkehlpieper
Pispola golarossa
Bisbita Gorgirrojo

2

Anthus trivialis
Tree Pipit
Pipit des arbres
Baumpieper
Prispolone
Bisbita Arbóreo

6

Anthus pratensis
Meadow Pipit
Pipit farlouse
Wiesenpieper
Pispola
Bisbita Común

3

Anthus campestris
Tawny Pipit
Pipit rousseline
Brachpieper
Calandro
Bisbita Campestre

7

Anthus spinoletta spinoletta
Water Pipit (Alpine Pipit)
Pipit spioncelle
Wasserpieper
Spioncello
Bisbita Ribereño Alpino

(S)

4

B, CH, F, N, P, S

Anthus novaeseelandiae
Richard's Pipit
Pipit de Richard
Spornpieper
Calandro maggiore
Bisbita de Richard

Pl. 12.

Rock Pipit.

Tawny Pipit.

Meadow-Pipit.

Richard's Pipit.

Tree-Pipit.

Red-throated Pipit.

Alpine Pipit.

13

(L)
ENGLISH
FRANÇAIS
DEUTSCH
ITALIANO
ESPAÑOL

1

Lanius collurio
Red-backed Shrike
Pie-grièche écorcheur
Neuntöter
Averla piccola
Alcaudón Dorsirrojo

♂ ♀

2

Lanius excubitor
Great Grey Shrike
Pie-grièche grise
Raubwürger
Averla maggiore
Alcaudón Real

3

Lanius senator
Woodchat Shrike
Pie-grièche à tête rousse
Rotkopfwürger
Averla capirossa
Alcaudón Común

4

Lanius nubicus
Masked Shrike
Pie-grièche masquée
Maskenwürger
Averla mascherata
Alcaudón Núbico

5

Lanius minor
Lesser Grey Shrike
Pie-grièche à poitrine rose
Schwarzstirnwürger
Averla cenerina
Alcaudón Chico

Pl. 13.

Red-backed Shrike. ♂ & ♀.   Great Grey Shrike

Woodchat Shrike   Masked Shrike   Lesser Grey Shrike

14

(L)
ENGLISH
FRANÇAIS
DEUTSCH
ITALIANO
ESPAÑOL

1

Muscicapa latirostris
Brown Flycatcher
Gobemouche brun
Braunschnäpper
Pigliamosche beccolargo
Papamoscas Pardo

DK, GB

2

Bombycilla garrulus
Waxwing
Jaseur boréal
Seidenschwanz
Beccofrusone
Ampelis Europeo

3

Muscicapa striata
Spotted Flycatcher
Gobemouche gris
Grauschnäpper
Pigliamosche
Papamoscas Gris

4

Ficedula parva
Red-breasted Flycatcher
Gobemouche nain
Zwergschnäpper
Pigliamosche pettirosso
Papamoscas Papirrojo

5

Ficedula hypoleuca
Pied Flycatcher
Gobemouche noir
Trauerschnäpper
Balia nera
Papamoscas Cerrojillo
♂ ♀

6

Ficedula albicollis
Collared Flycatcher
Gobemouche à collier
Halsbandschnäpper
Balia dal collare
Papamoscas Collarino

7

Oriolus oriolus
Golden Oriole
Loriot d'Europe
Pirol
Rigogolo
Oropéndola

Pl. 14

Waxwing.   Spotted Flycatcher.

Brown Flycatcher.

Pied Flycatcher.   Red-breasted Flycatcher.

Collared Flycatcher. Golden Oriole.

2

15

(L)
ENGLISH
FRANÇAIS
DEUTSCH
ITALIANO
ESPAÑOL

1

Hirundo daurica
Red-rumped Swallow
Hirondelle rousseline
Rötelschwalbe
Rondine rossiccia
Golondrina Dáurica

2

Riparia riparia
Sand Martin
Hirondelle de rivage
Uferschwalbe
Topino
Avión Zapador

3

Hirundo rustica
Swallow
Hirondelle de cheminée
Rauchschwalbe
Rondine
Golondrina Común

4

Carduelis spinus
Siskin
Tarin des aunes
Zeisig (Erlenzeisig)
Lucherino
Lúgano

5

Delichon urbica
House Martin (Martin)
Hirondelle de fenêtre
Mehlschwalbe
Balestruccio
Avión Común

o (J)

6

Carduelis carduelis
Goldfinch
Chardonneret
Stieglitz (Distelfink)
Cardellino
Jilguero

7

Coccothraustes coccothraustes
Hawfinch
Grosbec cassenoyaux
Kernbeisser
Frosone
Picogordo

8

Carduelis chloris
    (Chloris chloris)
Greenfinch
Verdier d'Europe
Grünling (Grünfink)
Verdone
Verderón Común

Pl. 15.

Red-rumped Swallow.   Sand-Martin.

Swallow.   Siskin.   Martin.

Goldfinch.   Hawfinch.   Greenfinch.

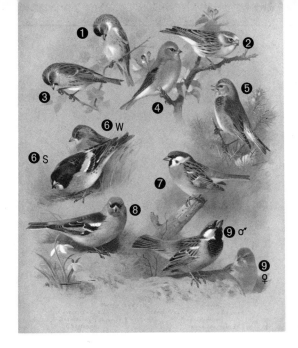

16

1

Carduelis flammea flammea
Redpoll (Mealy Redpoll)
Sizerin flammé
Birkenzeisig
Organetto
Pardillo Sizerín

2

Serinus serinus
Serin
Serin cini
Girlitz
Verzellino
Verdecillo

3

A, CH, F, GB, I

Carduelis flammea cabaret
Lesser Redpoll
Sizerin flammé des Alpes
Alpenbirkenzeisig
Organetto minore
Pardillo Sizerín Alpino

4

Serinus citrinella
Citril Finch
Venturon montagnard
Zitronengirlitz (Zitronenzeisig)
Venturone
Verderón Serrano

5

Carduelis cannabina
Linnet
Linotte mélodieuse
Hänfling
Fanello
Pardillo Común

6

Fringilla montifringilla
Brambling
Pinson du Nord
Bergfink
Peppola
Pinzón Real

(S) (W)

7

Passer montanus
Tree Sparrow
Moineau friquet
Feldsperling
Passera mattugia
Gorrión Molinero

8

Fringilla coelebs
Chaffinch
Pinson des arbres
Buchfink
Fringuello
Pinzón Vulgar

9

Passer domesticus
House Sparrow
Moineau domestique
Haussperling
Passera europea
Gorrión Común
♂ ♀

Pl. 16.

Mealy Redpoll.

Serin.

Lesser Redpoll.

Citril Finch.

Linnet.

Brambling (Summer & winter)

Tree Sparrow.

Chaffinch.

House Sparrow.

17

1

Miliaria calandra
  (Emberiza calandra)
Corn Bunting
Bruant proyer
Grauammer
Strillozzo
Triguero

2

Carduelis flavirostris
Twite
Linotte à bec jaune
Berghänfling
Fanello nordico
Pardillo Piquigualdo

3

Montifringilla nivalis
Snow Finch
Niverolle des Alpes
Schneefink
Fringuello alpino
Gorrión Alpino

(S)

4

Emberiza melanocephala
Black-headed Bunting
Bruant mélanocéphale
Kappenammer
Zigolo capinero
Escribano Cabecinegro

5

Emberiza leucocephalos
Pine Bunting
Bruant à calotte blanche
Fichtenammer
Zigolo golarossa
Escribano de Gmelin

(S)

6

Carpodacus erythrinus
Scarlet Rosefinch
  (Scarlet Grosbeak)
Roselin cramoisi
Karmingimpel
Ciuffolotto scarlatto
Camachuelo Carminoso

7

Pyrrhula pyrrhula
Bullfinch
Bouvreuil pivoine
Gimpel
Ciuffolotto
Camachuelo Común

♀ ♂

8

Loxia leucoptera
Two-barred Crossbill
Beccroisé bifascié
Bindenkreuzschnabel
Crociere fasciato
Piquituerto Franjeado

9

Pinicola enucleator
Pine Grosbeak
Durbec des sapins
Hakengimpel
Ciuffolotto delle pinete
Camachuelo Picogrueso

10

Loxia curvirostra
Crossbill
Beccroisé des sapins
Fichtenkreuzschnabel
Crociere
Piquituerto Común

Pl. 17.

Corn Bunting.
Black-headed Bunting.
Bullfinch (♂ ♀).

Twite.
Pine Bunting.
Two-barred Crossbill.
—Crossbill.

Snow-Finch.
Scarlet Grosbeak.
Pine Grosbeak.

18

6

Emberiza schoeniclus
Reed Bunting
Bruant des roseaux
Rohrammer
Migliarino di palude
Escribano Palustre

(S)

1

Emberiza rustica
Rustic Bunting
Bruant rustique
Waldammer
Zigolo boschereccio
Escribano Rústico

(S)

7

Calcarius lapponicus
Lapland Bunting
Bruant lapon
Spornammer
Zigolo di Lapponia
Escribano Lapón

2

Emberiza pusilla
Little Bunting
Bruant nain
Zwergammer
Zigolo minore
Escribano Pigmeo

8

GB, I

Emberiza cioides
Siberian Meadow Bunting
Bruant des prés
Wiesenammer
Zigolo muciatto orientale
Escribano de Brandt

(R)

3

Emberiza citrinella
Yellowhammer (Yellow Bunting)
Bruant jaune
Goldammer
Zigolo giallo
Escribano Cerillo

9

Emberiza cia
Rock Bunting (Meadow-Bunting)
Bruant fou
Zippammer
Zigolo muciatto
Escribano Montesino

4

Emberiza cirlus
Cirl Bunting
Bruant zizi
Zaunammer
Zigolo nero
Escribano Soteño

10

Plectrophenax nivalis
Snow Bunting
Bruant des neiges
Schneeammer
Zigolo delle nevi
Escribano Nival

♂(S) ♂(A)

5

Emberiza aureola
Yellow-breasted Bunting
Bruant auréole
Weidenammer
Zigolo dal collare
Escribano Aureolado

11

Emberiza hortulana
Ortolan Bunting (Ortolan)
Bruant ortolan
Ortolan
Ortolano
Escribano Hortelano

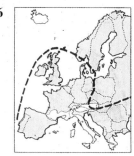

Pl. 18

Rustic Bunting.   Little Bunting.   Yellow Bunting or Yellow Hammer.
   Cirl Bunting. Yellow-breasted Bunting. Reed Bunting.   Lapland Bunting.
Siberian Meadow Bunting. Meadow-Bunting.   Snow-Bunting.
         Ortolan.   (Summer & Autumn)

19

(L)
ENGLISH
FRANÇAIS
DEUTSCH
ITALIANO
ESPAÑOL

1

Sturnus vulgaris
Starling
Etourneau sansonnet
Star
Storno
Estornino Pinto

(W) (S)

2

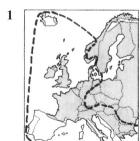

Sturnus roseus
Rose-coloured Starling
Martin roselin
Rosenstar
Storno roseo
Estornino Rosado

○ (J)

3

Nucifraga caryocatactes
Nutcracker
Cassenoix moucheté
Tannenhäher
Nocciolaia
Cascanueces

4

Pyrrhocorax pyrrhocorax
Chough
Crave à bec rouge
Alpenkrähe
Gracchio corallino
Chova Piquirroja

5

Garrulus glandarius
Jay
Geai des chênes
Eichelhäher
Ghiandaia
Arrendajo Común

Pl. 19.

Starling. (Summer & winter)   Rose-coloured Starling.
(adult & young)

Nutcracker   1
Jay.   3

Chough.

20

(L)
ENGLISH
FRANÇAIS
DEUTSCH
ITALIANO
ESPAÑOL

1

Pica pica
Magpie
Pie bavarde
Elster
Gazza
Urraca

2

Corvus corax
Raven
Grand Corbeau
Kolkrabe
Corvo imperiale
Cuervo

3

Corvus monedula
Jackdaw
Choucas des tours
Dohle
Taccola
Grajilla

(2x)

Pl. 20

Magpie.   Raven.   Jackdaw.

21

(L)
ENGLISH
FRANÇAIS
DEUTSCH
ITALIANO
ESPAÑOL

1

Corvus corone corone
Carrion Crow
Corneille noire
Rabenkrähe
Cornacchia nera
Corneja Negra

2

Corvus frugilegus
Rook
Corbeau freux
Saatkrähe
Corvo
Graja

3

Corvus corone cornix
Hooded Crow
Corneille mantelée
Nebelkrähe
Cornacchia grigia
Corneja Cenicienta

Pl. 21.

Carrion Crow.   Rook.   Hooded Crow.

22

(L)
ENGLISH
FRANÇAIS
DEUTSCH
ITALIANO
ESPAÑOL

1

Lullula arborea
Wood Lark
Alouette lulu
Heidelerche
Tottavilla
Totovía

2

Alauda arvensis
Sky Lark
Alouette des champs
Feldlerche
Allodola
Alondra Común

(2x)

3

Calandrella brachydactyla
    (cinerea)
Short-toed Lark
Alouette calandrelle
Kurzzehenlerche
Calandrella
Terrera Común

4

Eremophila alpestris
Shore Lark
Alouette hausse-col
Ohrenlerche
Allodola golagialla
Alondra Cornuda

5

GB, M, S

Melanocorypha leucoptera
White-winged Lark
Alouette leucoptère
Weissflügellerche
Calandra siberiana
Calandria Aliblanca

6

Galerida cristata
Crested Lark
Cochevis huppé
Haubenlerche
Cappellaccia
Cogujada Común

7

B, M, NL

Melanocorypha yeltoniensis
Black Lark
Alouette nègre
Mohrenlerche
Calandra nera
Calandria Negra
♂ (S) (W)

Pl. 22.

A. Thorburn 1914

Sky-Lark.   Wood Lark.
Shore-Lark.   Short-toed Lark.
Crested Lark.   White-winged Lark.
                              Black Lark (summer & winter)

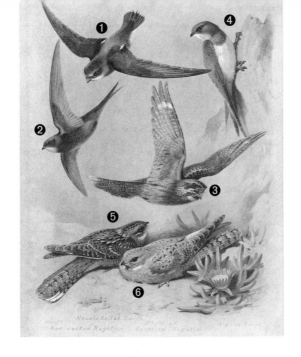

(L)
ENGLISH
FRANÇAIS
DEUTSCH
ITALIANO
ESPAÑOL

1

GB, I, IRL, SF

Hirundapus caudacutus
Needle-tailed Swift
Martinet à queue épineuse
Stachelschwanzsegler
Chetura codacuta
Rabitojo Mongol

(R)

4

Apus melba
Alpine Swift
Martinet à ventre blanc
Alpensegler
Rondone alpino
Vencejo Real

2

Apus apus
Swift
Martinet noir
Mauersegler
Rondone
Vencejo Común

5

Caprimulgus ruficollis
Red-necked Nightjar
Engoulevent à collier roux
Rothalsziegenmelker
Succiacapre collorosso
Chotacabras Pardo

3

Caprimulgus europaeus
Nightjar
Engoulevent d'Europe
Ziegenmelker (Nachtschwalbe)
Succiacapre
Chotacabras Gris

6

GB, I, M, S

Caprimulgus aegyptius
Egyptian Nightjar
Engoulevent du Sahara
Pharaonenziegenmelker
Succiacapre isabellino
Chotacabras Egipcio

Pl. 23.

Needle-tailed Swift.

Swift.   Nightjar.   Alpine Swift.

Red-necked Nightjar.   Egyptian Nightjar.

(L)
ENGLISH
FRANÇAIS
DEUTSCH
ITALIANO
ESPAÑOL

1

Jynx torquilla
Wryneck
Torcol fourmilier
Wendehals
Torcicollo
Torcecuello

2

Picus viridis
Green Woodpecker
Pic vert
Grünspecht
Picchio verde
Pito Real

3

Dendrocopos minor
Lesser Spotted Woodpecker
Pic épeichette
Kleinspecht
Picchio rosso minore
Pico Menor
♂ ♀

4

Dendrocopos major
Great Spotted Woodpecker
Pic épeiche
Buntspecht
Picchio rosso maggiore
Pico Picapinos
♂ (J)

5

Alcedo atthis
Kingfisher
Martin-pêcheur d'Europe
Eisvogel
Martin pescatore
Martín Pescador

6

Coracias garrulus
Roller
Rollier d'Europe
Blauracke
Ghiandaia marina
Carraca

Pl. 24.

Wryneck.

Green Woodpecker.

Lesser Spotted Woodpecker. ♂ & ♀.   Great Spotted Woodpecker. (adult ♂ & ♀ young).

Kingfisher.

Roller.

(L)
ENGLISH
FRANÇAIS
DEUTSCH
ITALIANO
ESPAÑOL

1

Cuculus canorus
Cuckoo
Coucou gris
Kuckuck
Cuculo
Cuco

○ (J)

2

A, CH, D, DK, E,
F, GB, P, SF

Clamator glandarius
Great Spotted Cuckoo
Coucou geai
Häherkuckuck
Cuculo dal ciuffo
Críalo

3

B, DK, F, GB, I, IS

Coccyzus americanus
Yellow-billed Cuckoo
  (American Yellow-billed
    Cuckoo)
Coulicou à bec jaune
Gelbschnabelkuckuck
Cuculo americano
Cuco Piquigualdo

4

Merops apiaster
Bee-eater
Guêpier d'Europe
Bienenfresser
Gruccione
Abejaruco Común

5

Upupa epops
Hoopoe
Huppe fasciée
Wiedehopf
Upupa
Abubilla

Pl. 25

Cuckoo. (adult & young). Great Spotted Cuckoo

American Yellow-billed Cuckoo. Bee-eater. Hoopoe.

$\frac{4}{9}$

1

Asio otus
Long-eared Owl
Hibou moyen-duc
Waldohreule
Gufo comune
Búho Chico

2

Strix aluco
Tawny Owl
Chouette hulotte
Waldkauz
Allocco
Cárabo Común

3

Tyto alba
Barn Owl
Chouette effraie
Schleiereule
Barbagianni
Lechuza Común

4

Asio flammeus
Short-eared Owl
Hibou des marais
Sumpfohreule
Gufo di palude
Lechuza Campestre

Pl. 26

Long-eared Owl.
Barn-Owl

Tawny Owl.
Short-eared Owl.

27

1

Otus scops
Scops Owl
Hibou petit-duc
Zwergohreule
Assiolo
Autillo

4

Athene noctua
Little Owl
Chouette chevêche
Steinkauz
Civetta
Mochuelo Común

2

Surnia ulula
Hawk Owl
Chouette épervière
Sperbereule
Ulula
Lechuza Gavilana

5

Nyctea scandiaca
Snowy Owl
Chouette harfang
Schnee-Eule
Gufo delle nevi
Búho Nival

♂ < ♀

3

Aegolius funereus
Tengmalm's Owl
Chouette de Tengmalm
Rauhfusskauz
Civetta capogrosso
Lechuza de Tengmalm

Pl. 27.

Scops Owl.

Hawk-Owl.   Tengmalm's Owl (with Dusky Warbler).
                                        Little Owl.
        Snowy Owl ♂   ⅓

28

1

Bubo bubo
Eagle Owl
Hibou grand-duc
Uhu
Gufo reale
Búho Real
♂ < ♀

Pl.28

Eagle-Owl.

29

(L)
ENGLISH
FRANÇAIS
DEUTSCH
ITALIANO
ESPAÑOL

1

Gyps fulvus
Griffon Vulture
Vautour fauve
Gänsegeier
Grifone
Buitre Común

2

Neophron percnopterus
Egyptian Vulture
Vautour percnoptère
Schmutzgeier
Capovaccaio
Alimoche Común

(J) ○

Pl. 29.

A. Thorburn
1914

Griffon Vulture
Egyptian Vulture. (adult & young)

5

30

(L)
ENGLISH
FRANÇAIS
DEUTSCH
ITALIANO
ESPAÑOL

1

Circus pygargus
Montagu's Harrier
Busard cendré
Wiesenweihe
Albanella minore
Aguilucho Cenizo
♂♀

2

Circus aeruginosus
Marsh Harrier
Busard des roseaux
Rohrweihe
Falco di palude
Aguilucho Lagunero
(J) ♂

3

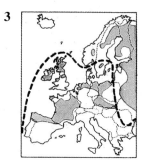

Circus cyaneus
Hen Harrier
Busard Saint-Martin
Kornweihe
Albanella reale
Aguilucho Pálido
♀♂

Pl. 30.

Montagu's Harrier ♂ & ♀.   Marsh Harrier ♂ ♀ & ♂ ♀.

A. Thorburn. 1914.

(L)
ENGLISH
FRANÇAIS
DEUTSCH
ITALIANO
ESPAÑOL

1

Buteo lagopus
Rough-legged Buzzard
Buse pattue
Rauhfussbussard
Poiana calzata
Ratonero Calzado

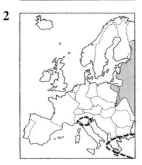

2

Aquila clanga
Spotted Eagle
Aigle criard
Schelladler
Aquila anatraia maggiore
Águila Moteada

(J)

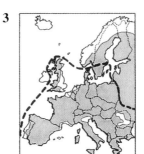

3

Buteo buteo
Buzzard (Common Buzzard)
Buse variable
Mäusebussard
Poiana
Ratonero Común

(2x)

Pl. 31.

Rough-legged Buzzard.   Spotted Eagle.   Common Buzzard.

32

(L)
ENGLISH
FRANÇAIS
DEUTSCH
ITALIANO
ESPAÑOL

1

Aquila chrysaetos
Golden Eagle
Aigle royal
Steinadler
Aquila reale
Águila Real

(J) ♂ < ♀

Pl. 32

Golden Eagle. (adult & young)

(L)
ENGLISH
FRANÇAIS
DEUTSCH
ITALIANO
ESPAÑOL

1

Haliaeetus albicilla
White-tailed Eagle
Pygargue à queue blanche
Seeadler
Aquila di mare
Pigargo

○ (J)

2

Pandion haliaetus
Osprey
Balbuzard pêcheur
Fischadler
Falco pescatore
Águila Pescadora

Pl. 33

A. Thorburn
1914.

White-tailed or Sea Eagle.
(adult & young)

Osprey.

$\frac{1}{5}$

34

(L)
ENGLISH
FRANÇAIS
DEUTSCH
ITALIANO
ESPAÑOL

1

Accipiter nisus
Sparrowhawk
Epervier d'Europe
Sperber
Sparviere
Gavilán
♀ ♂

2

Accipiter gentilis
Goshawk
Autour des palombes
Habicht
Astore
Azor
○ (J)

Pl. 34

Sparrow-Hawk. (♂ & ♀)

Goshawk (adult & young)

⅓.

(L)
ENGLISH
FRANÇAIS
DEUTSCH
ITALIANO
ESPAÑOL

1

Milvus migrans
Black Kite
Milan noir
Schwarzmilan
Nibbio bruno
Milano Negro

3

Pernis apivorus
Honey Buzzard
Bondrée apivore
Wespenbussard
Falco pecchiaiolo
Halcón Abejero

(2x)

2

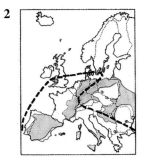

Milvus milvus
Red Kite (Kite)
Milan royal
Rotmilan
Nibbio reale
Milano Real

Pl. 35.

Black Kite.

Kite.

Honey-Buzzard. (2 varieties)

36

(L)
ENGLISH
FRANÇAIS
DEUTSCH
ITALIANO
ESPAÑOL

Falco rusticolus candicans
Greenland Gyrfalcon
  (Greenland Falcon)
Faucon gerfaut du Groenland
Weisser Gerfalke
Girfalco bianco
Halcón de Groenlandia
♀

Falco rusticolus islandus
Iceland Gyrfalcon
  (Iceland Falcon)
Faucon gerfaut d'Islande
Isländischer Gerfalke
Girfalco d'Islanda
Halcón de Islandia
♂

Pl. 36.

Greenland Falcon. ♀   Iceland Falcon. ♂

Falco rusticolus rusticolus
Gyrfalcon
Faucon gerfaut
Gerfalke
Girfalco
Halcón Gerifalte

♀

Falco peregrinus
Peregrine Falcon
Faucon pèlerin
Wanderfalke
Falco pellegrino
Halcón Común

(J) ○

Pl. 37.

Gyr-Falcon.
♀.

Peregrine Falcon (adult & young)
♂.

⅓.

38

1

Falco vespertinus
Red-footed Falcon
Faucon kobez
Rotfussfalke
Falco cuculo
Cernícalo Patirrojo
♂ ♀

4

Falco columbarius
Merlin
Faucon émerillon
Merlin
Smeriglio
Esmerejón
♀ (J) ♂

2

Falco subbuteo
Hobby
Faucon hobereau
Baumfalke
Lodolaio
Alcotán
♂

5

Falco tinnunculus
Kestrel
Faucon crécerelle
Turmfalke
Gheppio
Cernícalo Vulgar
♀ ♂

3

Falco naumanni
Lesser Kestrel
Faucon crécerellette
Rötelfalke
Falco grillaio
Cernícalo Primilla
♂

Pl. 38.

Hobby. ♂.
Merlin. (♂. ♀. & young).
Kestrel. ♀.

Red-footed Falcon. (♂. & ♀).
Lesser Kestrel. ♂.
Kestrel. ♂.

⅓

39

(L)
ENGLISH
FRANÇAIS
DEUTSCH
ITALIANO
ESPAÑOL

1

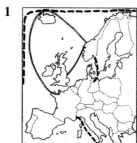

Sula bassana
Gannet
Fou de Bassan
Basstölpel
Sula
Alcatraz Común

○ (J)

2

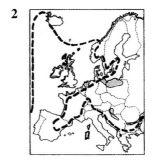

Phalacrocorax carbo
Cormorant
Grand Cormoran
Kormoran
Cormorano
Cormorán Grande

(J) ○

3

Phalacrocorax aristotelis
Shag
Cormoran huppé
Krähenscharbe
Marangone dal ciuffo
Cormorán Moñudo

(J) ○

Gannet. (adults & young)

Cormorant. (adult & young)

Shag. (adult & young)

40

1

Bubulcus ibis (Ardeola ibis)
Cattle Egret (Buff-backed Heron)
Héron gardebœuf
Kuhreiher
Airone guardabuoi
Garcilla Bueyera

2

Egretta garzetta
Little Egret
Aigrette garzette
Seidenreiher
Garzetta
Garceta Común

(S)

3

Ardea purpurea
Purple Heron
Héron pourpré
Purpurreiher
Airone rosso
Garza Imperial

4

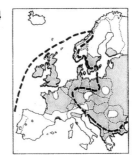

Ardea cinerea
Grey Heron (Common Heron)
Héron cendré
Graureiher
Airone cenerino
Garza Real

5

Egretta alba
Great White Egret
   (Great White Heron)
Grande Aigrette
Silberreiher
Airone bianco maggiore
Garceta Grande

Pl. 40.

A. Thorburn 1914.

Little Egret.

Buff-backed Heron.

Common Heron.

Purple Heron.

Great White Heron.

41

(L)
ENGLISH
FRANÇAIS
DEUTSCH
ITALIANO
ESPAÑOL

1

Nycticorax nycticorax
Night Heron
Héron bihoreau
Nachtreiher
Nitticora
Martinete

2

Plegadis falcinellus
Glossy Ibis
Ibis falcinelle
Sichler
Mignattaio
Morito

3

Ixobrychus minutus
Little Bittern
Blongios nain
Zwergdommel (Zwergreiher)
Tarabusino
Avetorillo Común

4

Ardeola ralloides
Squacco Heron
Héron crabier
Rallenreiher
Sgarza ciuffetto
Garcilla Cangrejera

5

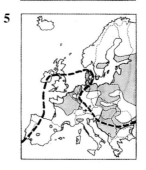

Botaurus stellaris
Bittern (Common Bittern)
Butor étoilé
Rohrdommel
Tarabuso
Avetoro Común

(2x)

6

F, GB, IRL, IS

Botaurus lentiginosus
American Bittern
Butor américain
Nordamerikanische Rohrdommel
Tarabuso americano
Avetoro Lentiginoso

Pl. 41.

Glossy Ibis.

Common Bittern.

Night-Heron.

Little Bittern. Squacco Heron.

American Bittern.

42

(L)
ENGLISH
FRANÇAIS
DEUTSCH
ITALIANO
ESPAÑOL

1

Platalea leucorodia
Spoonbill
Spatule blanche
Löffler
Spatola
Espátula

3

Ciconia ciconia
White Stork
Cigogne blanche
Weissstorch
Cicogna bianca
Cigüeña Común

2

Phoenicopterus ruber
Greater Flamingo (Flamingo)
Flamant rose
Flamingo
Fenicottero
Flamenco

4

Ciconia nigra
Black Stork
Cigogne noire
Schwarzstorch
Cicogna nera
Cigüeña Negra

Pl. 42.

Spoonbill.

White Stork.

Flamingo.

Black Stork.

$\frac{1}{6}$

43

(L)
ENGLISH
FRANÇAIS
DEUTSCH
ITALIANO
ESPAÑOL

1

Anser albifrons
White-fronted Goose
Oie rieuse
Blässgans
Oca lombardella
Ánsar Careto Grande

2

Anser anser
Greylag Goose
Oie cendrée
Graugans
Oca selvatica
Ánsar Común

3

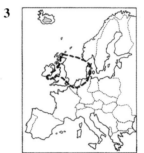

Anser brachyrhynchus
Pink-footed Goose
Oie à bec court
Kurzschnabelgans
Oca zamperosee
Ánsar Piquicorto

4

Anser fabalis
Bean Goose
Oie des moissons
Saatgans
Oca granaiola
Ánsar Campestre

Pl. 43.

A. Thorburn 1914

White-fronted Goose   Grey Lag-Goose.
Pink-footed Goose.   Bean-Goose.

4.

1

Brenta bernicla
Brent Goose
Bernache cravant
Ringelgans
Oca colombaccio
Barnacla Carinegra

2

Branta leucopsis
Barnacle Goose
Bernache nonnette
Nonnengans
Oca facciabianca
Barnacla Cariblanca

3

B, F, GB, IS, S

Branta ruficollis
Red-breasted Goose
Bernache à cou roux
Rothalsgans
Oca collorosso
Barnacla Cuellirroja

4

F, GB, IRL, IS

Anser caerulescens
Snow Goose
Oie des neiges
Schneegans
Oca delle nevi
Ánsar Nival

Pl. 44

Brent Goose.
Red-breasted Goose.

Bernacle Goose.
Snow Goose.

45

1

Cygnus columbianus
Bewick's Swan
Cygne de Bewick
Zwergschwan
Cigno minore
Cisne Chico

2

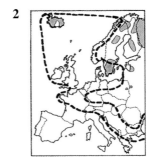

Cygnus cygnus
Whooper Swan
Cygne chanteur
Singschwan
Cigno selvatico
Cisne Cantor

(8x)

3

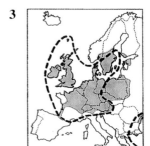

Cygnus olor
Mute Swan
Cygne tuberculé
Höckerschwan
Cigno reale
Cisne Vulgar

♀ (J)

Pl. 45.

Bewick's Swan. *Whooper Swan.*
Mute Swan (adult & young).

46

(L)
ENGLISH
FRANÇAIS
DEUTSCH
ITALIANO
ESPAÑOL

1

Anas platyrhynchos
Mallard
Canard colvert
Stockente
Germano reale
Ánade Real

♀ ♂

2

Anas strepera
Gadwall
Canard chipeau
Schnatterente
Canapiglia
Ánade Friso

♂ ♀

3

Tadorna ferruginea
Ruddy Shelduck
   (Ruddy Sheld-Duck)
Tadorne casarca
Rostgans
Casarca
Tarro Canelo

4

Tadorna tadorna
Shelduck (Common Sheld-Duck)
Tadorne de Belon
Brandgans (Brandente)
Volpoca
Tarro Blanco

Pl. 46.

Mallard (♂&♀)
Ruddy Sheld-Duck.

Gadwall. (♂&♀)
Common Sheld-Duck.

$\frac{1}{3}$

47

1

Anas crecca
Teal
Sarcelle d'hiver
Krickente
Alzavola
Cerceta Común
♀ ♂

4

Anas Crecca carolinensis
GB Green-winged Teal
   (American Green-winged Teal)
Sarcelle à ailes vertes
Amerikanische Krickente
Alzavola dalle ali verdi
Cerceta de Carolina
♂

2

Anas clypeata
Shoveler (Shoveller)
Canard souchet
Löffelente
Mestolone
Pato Cuchara
♂ ♀

5

Anas acuta
Pintail
Canard pilet
Spiessente
Codone
Ánade Rabudo
♀ ♂

3

DK, F, GB, I, IRL,
NL, S

Anas discors
Blue-winged Teal
   (American Blue-winged Teal)
Sarcelle soucrourou
Blauflügelente
Marzaiola americana
Cerceta Aliazul
♀ ♂

Pl. 47

Teal. (♂♀)   Shoveller (♂♀).
American Blue-winged Teal. (♂♀).   American Green-winged Teal.
Pintail (♂♀).

⅓

48

1

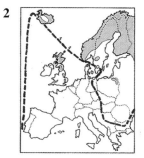

Aythya ferina
Pochard
Fuligule milouin
Tafelente
Moriglione
Porrón Común
♀ ♂

2

Anas penelope
Wigeon
Canard siffleur
Pfeifente
Fischione
Ánade Silbón
♂ ♀

3

Netta rufina
Red-crested Pochard
Nette rousse
Kolbenente
Fistione turco
Pato Colorado
♀ ♂

4

F, GB, IRL, NL

Anas americana
American Wigeon
Canard siffleur américain
Nordamerikanische Pfeifente
Fischione americano
Ánade Silbón Americano
♀ ♂

5

Anas querquedula
Garganey
Sarcelle d'été
Knäkente
Marzaiola
Cerceta Carretona
♂ ♀

Pl. 48.

Pochard. (♂&♀)

American Wigeon. (♂&♀)

Wigeon. (♂&♀)

Red-crested Pochard (♂&♀)

Garganey. (♂&♀)

A. Thorburn
1915

49

1

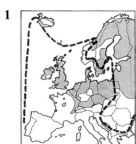

Aythya fuligula
Tufted Duck
Fuligule morillon
Reiherente
Moretta
Porrón Moñudo
♂ ♀

2

Aythya nyroca
Ferruginous Duck
Fuligule nyroca
Moorente
Moretta tabaccata
Porrón Pardo
♂ ♀

3

CS, GB, IS

Bucephala albeola
Bufflehead (Buffel-headed Duck)
Garrot albéole
Büffelkopfente
Quattrocchi minore
Porrón Albeola
♀ ♂
(R)

4

Bucephala clangula
Goldeneye
Garrot à œil d'or
Schellente
Quattrocchi
Porrón Osculado
♂ ♀

5

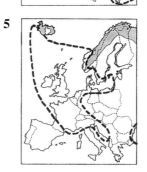

Aythya marila
Scaup (Scaup Duck)
Fuligule milouinan
Bergente
Moretta grigia
Porrón Bastardo
♂ ♀

6

Clangula hyemalis
Long-tailed Duck
Harelde de Miquelon
Eisente
Moretta codona
Havelda
♀, ♂ (W)

Pl. 49.

Tufted Duck. (♂♀)   Ferruginous Duck. (♂♀)
Buffel-headed Duck. (♂♀)   Golden-eye. (♂♀)   Scaup-Duck. (♂♀)
                    Long-tailed Duck. (♂♀)   ⅓

1

Histrionicus histrionicus
Harlequin (Harlequin Duck)
Garrot arlequin
Kragenente
Moretta arlecchino
Pato Arlequín
♀ ♂

D, GB, I, N, S

3

Somateria spectabilis
King Eider
Eider à tête grise
Prachteiderente
Re degli edredoni
Eider Real
♀ ♂

DK, F, GB, H, I,
IRL, N, IS

2

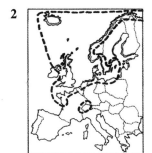

Somateria mollissima
Eider (Eider Duck)
Eider à duvet
Eiderente
Edredone
Eider
♂ ♀
(11x)

Pl. 50.

Harlequin Duck.(♂&♀)   Eider Duck.(♂&♀)

King-Eider.(♂&♀)

5.

51

1

Melanitta perspicillata
Surf Scoter
Macreuse à lunettes
B, D, F, GB, IS   Brillenente
Orco marino dagli occhiali
Negrón Careto
♂ ♀ ♂

2

Polysticta stelleri
Steller's Eider
Eider de Steller
D, F, GB, N   Scheckente
Edredone di Steller
Eider de Steller
♂ ♀

3

Melanitta nigra
Common Scoter
Macreuse noire
Trauerente
Orchetto marino
Negrón Común
♂ ♀

4

Melanitta fusca
Velvet Scoter
Macreuse brune
Samtente
Orco marino
Negrón Especulado
♂ ♀

Pl. 57

Surf. Scoter (♂♀).   Steller's Eider. (♂♀)
Common Scoter (♂♀).   Velvet Scoter. (♂♀).   3

52

(L)
ENGLISH
FRANÇAIS
DEUTSCH
ITALIANO
ESPAÑOL

1

Mergus serrator
Red-breasted Merganser
Harle huppé
Mittelsäger
Smergo minore
Serreta Mediana
♂♀♂

2

D, GB, IRL

Mergus cucullatus
Hooded Merganser
Harle couronné
Kappensäger
Smergo americano
Serreta Cabezona
♂ ♀
(R)

3

Mergus merganser
Goosander
Harle bièvre
Gänsesäger
Smergo maggiore
Serreta Grande
♀ ♂

4

Mergus albellus
Smew
Harle piette
Zwergsäger
Pesciaiola
Serreta Chica
♂ ♀

Pl. 52.

Red-breasted Merganser (♂♀).   Hooded Merganser (♂♀).
Goosander. (♂♀)   Smew (♂♀)

53

1

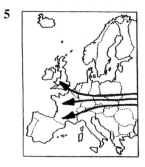

Columba palumbus
Woodpigeon
Pigeon ramier
Ringeltaube
Colombaccio
Paloma Torcaz

2

Columba oenas
Stock Dove
Pigeon colombin
Hohltaube
Colombella
Paloma Zurita

3

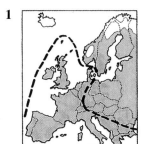

Streptopelia turtur
Turtle Dove
Tourterelle des bois
Turteltaube
Tortora
Tórtola Común

(2x)

4

Columba livia
Rock Dove
Pigeon biset
Felsentaube
Piccione selvatico
Paloma Bravía

(2x)

5

Syrrhaptes paradoxus
Pallas' Sandgrouse
Syrrhapte paradoxal
Steppenhuhn
Sirratte
Ganga de Pallas

(J) ♂♀♂♀

Pl. 53

Wood Pigeon   Stock Dove.
Turtle Dove. Pallas's Sand Grouse. (1849) Rock Dove.

⅓

54

(L)
ENGLISH
FRANÇAIS
DEUTSCH
ITALIANO
ESPAÑOL

1

Tetrao urogallus
Capercaillie
Grand Tétras
Auerhuhn
Gallo cedrone
Urogallo
♂ ♀

Pl. 54.

A. Thorburn. 1915.

Capercaillie (♂♀)

3

55

1

Lagopus lagopus scoticus
Red Grouse
Lagopède d'Ecosse
Schottisches Moorschneehuhn
Pernice bianca di Scozia
Lagópodo escocés

♂ (J) ♂ ♀

2

Tetrao tetrix
Black Grouse
Tétras lyre
Birkhuhn
Fagiano di monte
Gallo Lira

♀ ♀ ♂

Pl. 55.

A. Thorburn.
1915.

Red Grouse. (♂ & ♀)
Black Grouse. (♂ & ♀).

⅓

σ̅W

σ̅W

♀W

σ̅A

σ̅A

♀A

♀A

56

(L)
ENGLISH
FRANÇAIS
DEUTSCH
ITALIANO
ESPAÑOL

1

Lagopus mutus
Ptarmigan
Lagopède alpin
Alpenschneehuhn
Pernice bianca
Perdiz Nival
σ̅ ♀ σ̅ (W)
σ̅ ♀ ♀ σ̅ (A)

Pl. 56.

A. Thorburn
1915.

Ptarmigan (♂ ♀) winter & autumn.

57

1

Phasianus colchicus mongolicus
Mongolian Pheasant
Faisan du Turkestan
Mongolfasan
Fagiano mongolico
Faisán Mongol
♀♂

2

Phasianus colchicus colchicus
Pheasant
Faisan de Colchide
Fasan
Fagiano comune
Faisán Vulgar
♂♀

3

Phasianus versicolor
Japanese Pheasant
Faisan versicolore
Schillerfasan
Fagiano versicolore
Faisán japonés
♂

4

Phasianus colchicus torquatus
Grey-rumped Pheasant
   (Chinese Ring-necked
     Pheasant)
Faisan à collier
Ringfasan
Fagiano torquato
Faisán Chino
♂

Pl. 57.

Mongolian Pheasant. (♂♀).   Pheasant. (♂♀).   Japanese Pheasant.(♂).
Chinese Ring-necked Pheasant.(♂).

58

(L)
ENGLISH
FRANÇAIS
DEUTSCH
ITALIANO
ESPAÑOL

1

Perdix perdix
Partridge (Common Partridge)
Perdrix grise
Rebhuhn
Starna
Perdiz Pardilla
♂, ♀ (4x)

2

Alectoris rufa
Red-legged Partridge
Perdrix rouge
Rothuhn
Pernice rossa
Perdiz Común
♂ ♀

3

Coturnix coturnix
Quail
Caille des blés
Wachtel
Quaglia
Codorniz
♂ ♀

Pl. 58.

Common Partridge. (♂&♀)

Red-legged Partridge. (♂&♀)   Quail. (♂&♀)   ⅓

(L)
ENGLISH
FRANÇAIS
DEUTSCH
ITALIANO
ESPAÑOL

1

Fulica atra
Coot
Foulque macroule
Blässhuhn
Folaga
Focha Común

5

Porzana porzana
Spotted Crake
Marouette ponctuée
Tüpfelsumpfhuhn
Voltolino
Polluela Pintoja

2

Gallinula chloropus
Moorhen
Poule d'eau
Teichhuhn
Gallinella d'acqua
Polla de Agua

6

Porzana pusilla
Baillon's Crake
Marouette de Baillon
Zwergsumpfhuhn
Schiribilla grigiata
Polluela Chica

3

Rallus aquaticus
Water Rail
Râle d'eau
Wasserralle
Porciglione
Rascón

7

Porzana parva
Little Crake
Marouette poussin
Kleines Sumpfhuhn
Schiribilla
Polluela Bastarda

4

GB, IRL

Porzana carolina
Sora Rail (Carolina Crake)
Marouette de Caroline
Carolinasumpfhuhn
Voltolino americano
Polluela de la Carolina

(R)

8

Crex crex
Corncrake (Land Rail)
Râle de genêts
Wachtelkönig
Re di quaglie
Guión de Codornices

Pl.59.

½

Moor-hen.
Baillon's Crake.

Coot.
Water-Rail.
Little Crake.

Carolina Crake. Spotted Crake.
Land-Rail.

60

1

Otis tarda
Great Bustard
Outarde barbue
Grosstrappe
Otarda
Avutarda
♂ ♂ ♀
♀ ♀

Pl. 60.

Great Bustard. (♂ & ♀)

61

(L)
ENGLISH
FRANÇAIS
DEUTSCH
ITALIANO
ESPAÑOL

1

Burhinus oedicnemus
Stone Curlew
Oedicnème criard
Triel
Occhione
Alcaraván

2

Tetrax tetrax
Little Bustard
Outarde canepetière
Zwergtrappe
Gallina prataiola
Sisón
♀ ♂

3

B, CH, D, E, F,
GB, I

Chlamydotis undulata
Houbara Bustard
   (Macqueen's Bustard)
Outarde houbara
Kragentrappe
Ubara
Hubara

4

Grus grus
Crane
Grue cendrée
Kranich
Gru
Grulla Común

Pl. 61.

A. Thorburn. 1916.

Little Bustard. ♂♀.

Crane.

Stone. Curlew.

Macqeen's Bustard.

⅕

62

1

F, GB, I, IRL, N,
NL, S

Glareola nordmanni
Black-winged Pratincole
Glaréole à ailes noires
Schwarzflügelbrachschwalbe
Pernice di mare orientale
Canastera Alinegra

(2x)

2

Glareola pratincola
Pratincole
Glaréole à collier
Brachschwalbe
Pernice di mare
Canastera

(2x)

3

F, GB, I

Charadrius asiaticus
Caspian Plover
Pluvier asiatique
Wermutregenpfeifer
Corriere asiatico
Chorlitejo Asiático

(J) ○

4

B, D, E, F, GB, I,
N, S, SF

Cursorius cursor
Cream-coloured Courser
Courvite isabelle
Rennvogel
Corrione biondo
Corredor

5

Charadrius hiaticula
Ringed Plover
Grand Gravelot
Sandregenpfeifer
Corriere grosso
Chorlitejo Grande

6

Eudromias (Charadrius)
morinellus
Dotterel
Pluvier guignard
Mornellregenpfeifer
Piviere tortolino
Chorlito Carambolo

7

Charadrius dubius
Little Ringed Plover
Petit Gravelot
Flussregenpfeifer
Corriere piccolo
Chorlitejo Chico

8

Charadrius alexandrinus
Kentish Plover
Gravelot à collier interrompu
Seeregenpfeifer
Fratino
Chorlitejo Patinegro

Pl. 62

Black-winged Pratincole.   Pratincole.
Caspian Plover. (adult & young). Cream-coloured Courser.   2
          Dotterel.   Little Ringed Plover.   Ringed Plover.   5

63

(L)
ENGLISH
FRANÇAIS
DEUTSCH
ITALIANO
ESPAÑOL

1

B, D, DK, E, GB, IRL, SF

Chettusia gregaria
Sociable Lapwing (Sociable Plover)
Vanneau sociable
Steppenkiebitz
Pavoncella gregaria
Chorlito Social

(J), o (S)

4

E, F, GB, I

Pluvialis dominica
Lesser Golden Plover
(Asiatic Golden Plover)
Pluvier doré asiatique
Kleiner Goldregenpfeifer
Piviere asiatico
Chorlito Dorado Chico

2

CH, F, GB, IRL, IS, N

Charadrius vociferus
Killdeer (Killdeer Plover)
Gravelot kildir
Keilschwanzregenpfeifer
Corriere americano
Chorlitejo Culirrojo

5

Pluvialis squatarola
Grey Plover
Pluvier argenté
Kiebitzregenpfeifer
Pivieressa
Chorlito Gris

(W) (S)

3

Pluvialis apricaria
Golden Plover
Pluvier doré
Goldregenpfeifer
Piviere dorato
Chorlito Dorado Común

(W) (S)

6

Vanellus vanellus
Lapwing
Vanneau huppé
Kiebitz
Pavoncella
Avefría

Pl. 63

Sociable Plover. (adult & young)

Golden Plover. (summer & winter).

Grey Plover. (summer & winter).

Killdeer Plover.

Asiatic Golden Plover.

Lapwing.

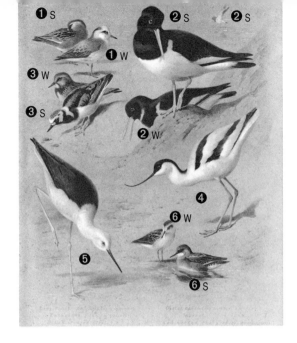

64

(L)
ENGLISH
FRANÇAIS
DEUTSCH
ITALIANO
ESPAÑOL

1

Phalaropus fulicarius
Grey Phalarope
Phalarope à bec large
Thorshühnchen
Falaropo beccolargo
Falaropo Picogrueso

(S) (W)

2

Haematopus ostralegus
Oystercatcher
Huîtrier pie
Austernfischer
Beccaccia di mare
Ostrero

(W), (S) (2x)

3

Arenaria interpres
Turnstone
Tournepierre à collier
Steinwälzer
Voltapietre
Vuelvepiedras

(S) (W)

4

Recurvirostra avosetta
Avocet
Avocette
Säbelschnäbler
Avocetta
Avoceta

5

Himantopus himantopus
Black-winged Stilt
Echasse blanche
Stelzenläufer
Cavaliere d'Italia
Cigüeñuela

6

Phalaropus lobatus
Red-necked Phalarope
Phalarope à bec étroit
Odinshühnchen
Falaropo beccosottile
Falaropo Picofino

(W) (S)

Grey Phalarope. (winter & summer).   Oyster.catcher. (summer & winter).

Turnstone. (summer & winter).   Avocet.

Black.winged Stilt.   Red.necked Phalarope (summer & winter)

3

65

1

Gallinago gallinago
Snipe (Common Snipe)
Bécassine des marais
Bekassine
Beccaccino
Agachadiza Común

(2x)

2

Scolopax rusticola
Woodcock
Bécasse des bois
Waldschnepfe
Beccaccia
Chocha Perdiz

3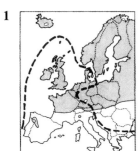

Lymnocryptes minimus
Jack Snipe
Bécassine sourde
Zwergschnepfe
Frullino
Agachadiza Chica

4

Gallinago media
Great Snipe
Bécassine double
Doppelschnepfe
Croccolone
Agachadiza Real

5

Limicola falcinellus
Broad-billed Sandpiper
Bécasseau falcinelle
Sumpfläufer
Gambecchio frullino
Correlimos Falcinelo

6

Xenus cinereus
Terek Sandpiper
Bargette du Térek
Terekwasserläufer
Piro-piro terek
Andarríos del Terek

7

F, GB, IRL

Calidris melanotos
Pectoral Sandpiper
Bécasseau tacheté
Graubruststrandläufer
Piro-piro pettorale
Correlimos Pectoral

8

F, GB

Calidris bairdii
Baird's Sandpiper
Bécasseau de Baird
Bairdstrandläufer
Gambecchio di Baird
Correlimos de Baird

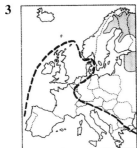

Common Snipe.   Woodcock.

Jack Snipe.   Great Snipe.

Broad-billed Sandpiper.   Terek Sandpiper.   Pectoral Sandpiper.   Baird's Sandpiper.

2/5

66

(L)
ENGLISH
FRANÇAIS
DEUTSCH
ITALIANO
ESPAÑOL

1

Calidris alba
Sanderling
Bécasseau sanderling
Sanderling
Piovanello tridattilo
Correlimos Tridáctilo

(S) (W)

2

Calidris alpina
Dunlin
Bécasseau variable
Alpenstrandläufer
Piovanello pancianera
Correlimos Común

(W) (S)

3

F, GB

Calidris fuscicollis
White-rumped Sandpiper
(Bonaparte's Sandpiper)
Bécasseau de Bonaparte
Weissbürzelstrandläufer
Piro-piro dorsobianco
Correlimos de Bonaparte

4

Calidris minuta
Little Stint
Bécasseau minute
Zwergstrandläufer
Gambecchio
Correlimos Menudo

(A) (S)

5

Calidris canutus
Knot
Bécasseau maubèche
Knutt
Piovanello maggiore
Correlimos Gordo

(S) (W)

6

Calidris temminckii
Temminck's Stint
Bécasseau de Temminck
Temminckstrandläufer
Gambecchio nano
Correlimos de Temminck

7

Calidris maritima
Purple Sandpiper
Bécasseau violet
Meerstrandläufer
Piovanello violetto
Correlimos Oscuro

(S) (W)

8

F, GB

Calidris minutilla
Least Sandpiper (American Stint)
Bécasseau minuscule
Wiesenstrandläufer
Gambecchio americano
Correlimos Menudillo

9

Calidris ferruginea
Curlew Sandpiper
Bécasseau cocorli
Sichelstrandläufer
Piovanello
Correlimos Zarapitín

(S) (A)

Pl. 66

Sanderling (winter & summer).   Dunlin. (winter & summer).
Bonaparte's Sandpiper.   Little Stint (summer & autumn)
                              Knot. (winter & summer).
                                                                          Temminck's Stint.
Purple Sandpiper (winter & summer)   American Stint.
                                                                  Curlew Sandpiper (summer & autumn)

⅔

(L)
ENGLISH
FRANÇAIS
DEUTSCH
ITALIANO
ESPAÑOL

1

Actitis hypoleucos
Common Sandpiper
Chevalier guignette
Flussuferläufer
Piro-piro piccolo
Andarríos Chico

2

B, CH, D, GB, IRL

Actitis macularia
Spotted Sandpiper
Chevalier grivelé
Drosseluferläufer
Piro-piro macchiato
Andarríos Maculado

3

Tringa glareola
Wood Sandpiper
Chevalier sylvain
Bruchwasserläufer
Piro-piro boschereccio
Andarríos Bastardo

4

F, GB

Tryngites subruficollis
Buff-breasted Sandpiper
Bécasseau rousset
Grasläufer
Piro-piro fulvo
Correlimos Canelo

5

D, DK, F, GB, I, M, NL

Bartramia longicauda
Upland Sandpiper
  (Bartram's Sandpiper)
Maubèche des champs
Prärieläufer
Piro-piro codalunga
Correlimos de Bartram

6

F, GB

Calidris pusilla
Semipalmated Sandpiper
Bécasseau semi-palmé
Sandstrandläufer
Piro-piro semipalmato
Correlimos Semipalmeado

7

Philomachus pugnax
Ruff
Combattant varié
Kampfläufer
Combattente
Combatiente
♂♀ ♂♂

Pl. 67

Common Sandpiper.   Spotted Sandpiper.   Wood-Sandpiper.

　　　Buff-breasted Sandpiper.   Bartram's Sandpiper.

Semi-palmated Sandpiper.   2／5.

　　　　　　Ruff.   Reeve.

68

(L)
ENGLISH
FRANÇAIS
DEUTSCH
ITALIANO
ESPAÑOL

1

Tringa ochropus
Green Sandpiper
Chevalier culblanc
Waldwasserläufer
Piro-piro culbianco
Andarríos Grande

2

Tringa erythropus
Spotted Redshank
Chevalier arlequin
Dunkler Wasserläufer
Totano moro
Archibebe Oscuro

(S) (W)

3

Tringa totanus
Redshank
Chevalier gambette
Rotschenkel
Pettegola
Archibebe Común

4

Tringa nebularia
Greenshank
Chevalier aboyeur
Grünschenkel
Pantana
Archibebe Claro

5

DK, E, GB, IRL, N

Limnodromus griseus
Short-billed Dowitcher
(Red-breasted Snipe)
Limnodrome à bec court
Kurzschnabel-Schlammläufer
Piro-piro Pettorossiccio minore
Agujeta Gris

6

Tringa stagnatilis
Marsh Sandpiper
Chevalier stagnatile
Teichwasserläufer
Albastrello
Archibebe Fino

7

F, GB, IRL, IS

Tringa solitaria
Solitary Sandpiper
Chevalier solitaire
Einsiedelwasserläufer
Piro-piro solitario
Andarríos Solitario

8

GB, IRL, IS

Tringa melanoleuca
Greater Yellowlegs
(Greater Yellowshank)
Grand Chevalier à pattes jaunes
Grosser Gelbschenkel
Totano zampegialle maggiore
Archibebe Patigualdo Grande

Pl. 68

Green Sandpiper.   Spotted Redshank. (summer & winter)

Redshank.

Greenshank.   Red-breasted Snipe.   Marsh. Sandpiper.   ⅔

Solitary Sandpiper.   Greater Yellowshank.

69

(L)
ENGLISH
FRANÇAIS
DEUTSCH
ITALIANO
ESPAÑOL

1

Limosa lapponica
Bar-tailed Godwit
Barge rousse
Pfuhlschnepfe
Pittima minore
Aguja Colipinta

(W) (S)

2

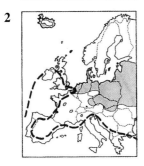

Limosa limosa
Black-tailed Godwit
Barge à queue noire
Uferschnepfe
Pittima reale
Aguja Colinegra

(W) (S)

3

GB, IRL, N

Numenius borealis
Eskimo Curlew
Courlis esquimau
Eskimobrachvogel
Chiurlo boreale
Zarapito Esquimal

(R)

4

Numenius tenuirostris
Slender-billed Curlew
Courlis à bec grêle
Dünnschnabelbrachvogel
Chiurlottello
Zarapito Fino

5

Numenius phaeopus
Whimbrel
Courlis corlieu
Regenbrachvogel
Chiurlo piccolo
Zarapito Trinador

6

Numenius arquata
Curlew (Common Curlew)
Courlis cendré
Grosser Brachvogel
Chiurlo
Zarapito Real

Pl. 69.

Bar-tailed Godwit. (summer & winter)   Black-tailed Godwit. (summer & winter)
Eskimo Curlew.   Slender-billed Curlew.
Whimbrel.   Common Curlew.

70

(L)
ENGLISH
FRANÇAIS
DEUTSCH
ITALIANO
ESPAÑOL

1

Chlidonias hybrida
Whiskered Tern
Guifette moustac
Weissbartseeschwalbe
Mignattino piombato
Fumarel Cariblanco

(J) ○

2

Chlidonias leucopterus
White-winged Black Tern
Guifette leucoptère
Weissflügelseeschwalbe
Mignattino alibianche
Fumarel Aliblanco

○ (J)

3

Chlidonias niger
Black Tern
Guifette noire
Trauerseeschwalbe
Mignattino
Fumarel Común

4

D, E, F, GB, I, S

Sterna fuscata
Sooty Tern
Sterne fuligineuse
Russseeschwalbe
Sterna scura
Charrán Sombrío

5

Gelochelidon nilotica
Gull-billed Tern
Sterne hansel
Lachseeschwalbe
Sterna zampenere
Pagaza Piconegra

○ (J)

6

Sterna caspia
Caspian Tern
Sterne caspienne
Raubseeschwalbe
Sterna maggiore
Pagaza Piquirroja

(S)

Pl. 70.

Whiskered Tern. (adult & young).   White-winged Black Tern. (adult & young).

Black Tern.

Sooty Tern.   Gull-billed Tern (adult & young). 2/7

Caspian Tern.

(L)
ENGLISH
FRANÇAIS
DEUTSCH
ITALIANO
ESPAÑOL

1

Sterna dougallii
Roseate Tern
Sterne de Dougall
Rosenseeschwalbe
Sterna del Dougall
Charrán Rosado

(J) ○

2

Sterna paradisaea
Arctic Tern
Sterne arctique
Küstenseeschwalbe
Sterna codalunga
Charrán Ártico

○ (J)

3

Sterna hirundo
Common Tern
Sterne pierregarin
Flussseeschwalbe
Sterna commune
Charrán Común

○ (J)

4

Sterna sandvicensis
Sandwich Tern
Sterne caugek
Brandseeschwalbe
Beccapesci
Charrán Patinegro

(J) ○

5

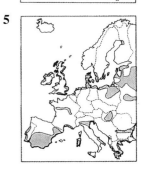

Sterna albifrons
Little Tern
Sterne naine
Zwergseeschwalbe
Fraticello
Charrancito

○ (J)

Pl. 71

Roseate Tern.   Arctic Tern.

                                 Common Tern.

Sandwich Tern.   Little Tern.

(Adults & young.)

72

1

D, DK, F, GB, I,
IRL, NL

Rhodostethia rosea
Ross' Gull
Mouette de Ross
Rosenmöwe
Gabbiano di Ross
Gaviota de Ross

(W) (S)

2

CH, E, F, GB, SF

Larus sabini
Sabine's Gull
Mouette de Sabine
Schwalbenmöwe
Gabbiano di Sabine
Gaviota de Sabine

3

Larus canus
Common Gull
Goéland cendré
Sturmmöwe
Gavina
Gaviota Cana

(J) ○

4

B, F, GB, IRL, IS,
N, NL

Larus philadelphia
Bonaparte's Gull
Mouette de Bonaparte
Bonaparte-Möwe
Gabbiano di Bonaparte
Gaviota de Bonaparte

5

Larus melanocephalus
Mediterranean Gull
    (Mediterranean Black-
    headed Gull)
Mouette mélanocéphale
Schwarzkopfmöwe
Gabbiano corallino
Gaviota Cabecinegra

6

Larus minutus
Little Gull
Mouette pygmée
Zwergmöwe
Gabbianello
Gaviota Enana

(J) ○

7

Larus ridibundus
Black-headed Gull
Mouette rieuse
Lachmöwe
Gabbiano comune
Gaviota Reidora

(S) (W)

Pl. 72.

Ross's Gull. (summer & winter).   Sabine's Gull.
      Common Gull. (adult & young).   Bonaparte's Gull.
  Mediterranean Black-headed Gull.
      Little Gull (adult & young).   Black-headed Gull. (summer & winter).

73

1

Larus argentatus
Herring Gull
Goéland argenté
Silbermöwe
Gabbiano reale
Gaviota Argéntea

(J) o

2

Larus fuscus
Lesser Black-backed Gull
Goéland brun
Heringsmöwe
Zafferano
Gaviota Sombría

3

F, GB, I, IS, N, S

Larus glaucoides
Iceland Gull
Goéland à ailes blanches
Polarmöwe
Gabbiano d'Islanda
Gaviota Polar

4

B, DK, GB, I, M,
NL, S

Larus ichthyaetus
Great Black-headed Gull
Goéland à tête noire
Fischmöwe
Gabbiano del Pallas
Gavión Cabecinegro

Pl. 7.

A. Thorburn
1915.

Herring-Gull. (adult & young).
Lesser Black-backed Gull.
Iceland Gull.   Great Black-headed Gull.

1/4.

74

1

Rissa tridactyla
Kittiwake (Kittiwake Gull)
Mouette tridactyle
Dreizehenmöwe
Gabbiano tridattilo
Gaviota Tridáctila

○ (J)

2

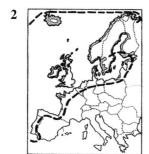

Larus marinus
Great Black-backed Gull
Goéland marin
Mantelmöwe
Mugnaiaccio
Gavión

○ (J)

3

F, GB, I, IS, N, S

Pagophila eburnea
Ivory Gull
Mouette ivoire
Elfenbeinmöwe
Gabbiano d'avorio
Gaviota Marfil

4

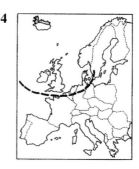

Larus hyperboreus
Glaucous Gull
Goéland bourgmestre
Eismöwe
Gabbiano glauco
Gaviota Hiperbórea

Pl. 74.

Kittiwake Gull. (adult & young).

Great Black-backed Gull. (adult & young).

Ivory Gull.

Glaucous Gull.

(L)
ENGLISH
FRANÇAIS
DEUTSCH
ITALIANO
ESPAÑOL

1

Stercorarius parasiticus
Arctic Skua (Richardson's Skua)
Labbe parasite
Schmarotzerraubmöwe
Labbo
Págalo Parásito

(2x)

2

D, E, F, GB, H, I,
N, S, YU

Stercorarius skua
Great Skua
Grand Labbe
Skua
Stercorario maggiore
Págalo Grande

(2x)

3

Stercorarius pomarinus
Pomarine Skua
        (Pomatorine Skua)
Labbe pomarin
Spatelraubmöwe
Stercorario mezzano
Págalo Pomarino

(2x)

4

Stercorarius longicaudus
Long-tailed Skua (Buffon's Skua)
Labbe à longue queue
Falkenraubmöwe
Labbo codalunga
Págalo Rabero

Pl. 75.

Richardson's Skua.　　　　　　Great Skua.
Pomatorine Skua.　　　Long-tailed or Buffon's Skua.

4

(L)
ENGLISH
FRANÇAIS
DEUTSCH
ITALIANO
ESPAÑOL

1

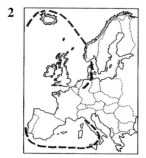

Cepphus grylle
Black Guillemot
Guillemot à miroir
Gryllteiste
Uria nera
Arao Aliblanco

(S) (W)

2

Fratercula arctica
Puffin
Macareux moine
Papageitaucher
Pulcinella di mare
Frailecillo Común

(W) (S)

3

Uria aalge
Guillemot (Common Guillemot)
Guillemot de Troïl
Trottellumme
Uria
Arao Común

(2x)

4

A, CS, F, GB, IS, N

Uria lomvia
Brünnich's Guillemot
Guillemot de Brünnich
Dickschnabellumme
Uria di Brünnich
Arao de Brünnich

(W)

5

Alca torda
Razorbill
Pingouin torda
Tordalk
Gazza marina
Alca Común

(W) (S)

6

Pinguinus impennis
Great Auk
Grand Pingouin
Riesenalk
Pinguino
Pingüino

(†)

7

D, DK, E, F, GB, I,
S, SF

Alle alle
Little Auk
Mergule nain
Krabbentaucher
Gazza marina minore
Mérgulo Marino

(S) (W)

Pl. 76.

Black Guillemot. (summer & winter).
Common Guillemot.
Razorbill (summer & winter)
Great Auk.

Puffin. (summer & winter)
Brünnich's Guillemot.

Little Auk. (summer & winter)

(L)
ENGLISH
FRANÇAIS
DEUTSCH
ITALIANO
ESPAÑOL

1

Gavia immer
Great Northern Diver
Plongeon imbrin
Eistaucher
Strolaga maggiore
Colimbo Grande

(S) (W)

2

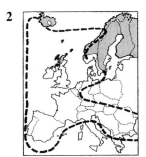

Gavia stellata
Red-throated Diver
Plongeon catmarin
Sterntaucher
Strolaga minore
Colimbo Chico

(W) (S)

3

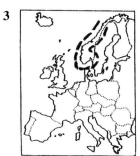

Gavia adamsii
White-billed Diver
    (White-billed Northern Diver)
Plongeon à bec blanc
Gelbschnabel-Eistaucher
Strolaga beccogiallo
Colimbo de Adams

(S)

4

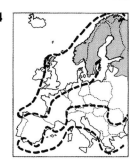

Gavia arctica
Black-throated Diver
Plongeon arctique
Prachttaucher
Strolaga mezzana
Colimbo Ártico

(S)

Pl. 77.

Red-throated Diver. (summer & winter)

Great Northern Diver (summer & winter).

White-billed Northern Diver.

Black-throated Diver.

5.

(L)
ENGLISH
FRANÇAIS
DEUTSCH
ITALIANO
ESPAÑOL

1

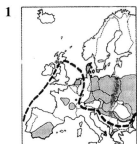

Podiceps nigricollis
Black-necked Grebe (Eared Grebe)
Grèbe à cou noir
Schwarzhalstaucher
Svasso piccolo
Zampullín Cuellinegro

(S)

2

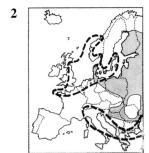

Podiceps grisegena
Red-necked Grebe
Grèbe jougris
Rothalstaucher
Svasso collorosso
Somormujo Cuellirrojo

(S)

3

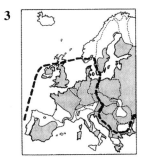

Podiceps cristatus
Great Crested Grebe
Grèbe huppé
Haubentaucher
Svasso maggiore
Somormujo Lavanco

(S)

4

Podiceps auritus
Slavonian Grebe (Horned Grebe)
Grèbe esclavon
Ohrentaucher
Svasso cornuto
Zampullín Cuellirrojo

(W) (S)

5

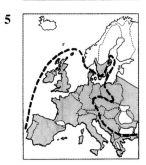

Tachybaptus ruficollis
Little Grebe
Grèbe castagneux
Zwergtaucher
Tuffetto
Zampullín Chico

(S) (W)

Pl. 78.

Black-necked or Eared Grebe.

Red-necked Grebe.   Great Crested Grebe. $\frac{1}{3}$

Slavonian or Horned Grebe. (summer & winter)   Little Grebe. (summer & winter).

(L)
ENGLISH
FRANÇAIS
DEUTSCH
ITALIANO
ESPAÑOL

1

Hydrobates pelagicus
Storm Petrel
Pétrel tempête
Sturmschwalbe
Uccello delle tempeste
Paíño Común

2

Oceanodroma leucorhoa
Leach's Petrel
   (Leach's Fork-tailed Petrel)
Pétrel culblanc
Wellenläufer
Uccello delle tempeste codaforcuta
Paíño de Leach

3

GB, IRL

Pelagodroma marina
Frigate Petrel
Pétrel frégate
Fregattensturmschwalbe
Uccello delle tempeste fregata
Paíño Pechialbo
(R)

4

E, GB, IRL

Oceanodroma castro
Madeiran Petrel
   (Madeiran Fork-tailed Petrel)
Pétrel de Castro
Madeira-Wellenläufer
Uccello delle tempeste di Castro
Paíño de Madeira
(R)

5

F, GB, IRL

Oceanites oceanicus
Wilson's Petrel
Pétrel océanite
Buntfusssturmschwalbe
Uccello delle tempeste di Wilson
Paíño de Wilson

6

Puffinus griseus
Sooty Shearwater
Puffin fuligineux
Dunkler Sturmtaucher
Berta grigia
Pardela Sombría

7

D, DK, E, F, GB,
IS, P

Puffinus assimilis
Little Shearwater
   (Little Dusky Shearwater)
Petit Puffin (Puffin obscur)
Kleiner Sturmtaucher
Berta minore fosca
Pardela Chica

8

Puffinus gravis
Great Shearwater
Puffin majeur
Grosser Sturmtaucher
Berta dell'Atlantico
Pardela Capirotada

Pl. 79.

A. Thorburn 1916.

Storm Petrel.   Leach's Fork-tailed Petrel.
Frigate Petrel.   Madeiran Fork-tailed Petrel.
Wilson's Petrel.   Sooty Shearwater.
Little Dusky Shearwater.   Great Shearwater.

80

1

Puffinus puffinus
Manx Shearwater
Puffin des Anglais
Schwarzschnabelsturmtaucher
Berta minore
Pardela Pichoneta

2

GB, IRL, IS, N

Diomedea melanophris
Black-browed Albatross
Albatros à sourcils noirs
Mollymauk
Albatro a sopracciglio nero
Albatros Ojeroso

3

F, GB

Pterodroma hasitata
Capped Petrel
Pétrel diablotin
Teufelssturmvogel
*Uccello delle tempeste
   dal cappuccio
      (Berta dal cappucio)*
Petrel Antillano

(R)

4

GB, I

Pterodroma leucoptera
Collared Petrel
Pétrel à ailes blanches
Brustbandsturmvogel
Uccello delle tempeste dal collare
Petrel de Gould

(R)

5

GB, I

Bulweria bulwerii
Bulwer's Petrel
Pétrel de Bulwer
Bulwersturmvogel
Uccello delle tempeste di Bulwer
Petrel de Bulwer

6

Fulmarus glacialis
Fulmar
Pétrel fulmar (Fulmar)
Eissturmvogel
Fulmaro
Fulmar

7

GB

Pterodroma neglecta
Kermadec Petrel
   (Schlegel's Petrel)
Pétrel de Kermadec
Kermadecsturmvogel
*Uccello delle tempeste
   di Kermadec*
Petrel de Kermadec

(R)

Pl. 80.

Black-browed Albatross. (scale ½.)   Manx Shearwater.   Capped Petrel.

Collared Petrel.

Fulmar.   Bulwer's Petrel.   ⅓

Schlegel's Petrel.

BIBLIOGRAPHY

R. PETERSON, G. MOUNTFORT, P.A.D. HOLLOM, *A Field Guide to the Birds of Britain and Europe.* Collins, London.

J.T.R. SHARROCK, *The Atlas of Breeding Birds in Britain and Ireland.* British Trust for Ornithology, Irish Wildbird Conservancy. Published by T. & A.D. Poyser Ltd, Calton, Staffordshire.

A. THORBURN, *British Birds.* Longmans, Green and Co, London.

K.H. WOOUS, *List of Recent Holarctic Bird Species.* Ibis 115, 1973 and Ibis 119, 1977.

BIBLIOGRAPHIE

H. HEINZEL, R. FITTER, J. PARSLOW, *Oiseaux d'Europe, d'Afrique du Nord et du Moyen-Orient.* Adaptation française : M. Cuisin. Delachaux et Niestlé S.A., Neuchâtel, Paris.

CH. PERRINS, M. CUISIN, *Les oiseaux d'Europe.* Delachaux et Niestlé S.A., Neuchâtel, Paris.

R. PETERSON, G. MOUNTFORT, P.A.D. HOLLOM, *Guide des oiseaux d'Europe.* Adaptation française : P. Géroudet. Delachaux et Niestlé S.A., Neuchâtel, Paris.

L. YEATMAN, *Atlas des oiseaux nicheurs de France.* Société Ornithologique de France, Paris.

LITERATUR

G. NIETHAMMER, H. KRAMER, H.E. WOLTERS, *Die Vögel Deutschlands (Artenliste).* Akademische Verlagsgesellschaft, Frankfurt am Main.

R. PETERSON, G. MOUNTFORT, P.A.D. HOLLOM, *Die Vögel Europas.* Übersetzt und bearbeitet von Prof. Dr. G. Niethammer. Verlag Paul Parey, Hamburg und Berlin.

A. SCHIFFERLI, P. GÉROUDET, R. WINKLER, *Verbreitungsatlas der Brutvögel der Schweiz.* Schweizerische Vogelwarte, Sempach.

R. WINKLER, *Liste der Vogelarten der Schweiz.* Der Ornithologische Beobachter 86, Heft 3.

BIBLIOGRAFIA

G. BOLOGNA, *Uccelli.* Arnoldo Mondadori Editore S.p.A., Milano.

B. BRUUN, A. SINGER, *Uccelli d'Europa.* Arnoldo Mondadori Editore S.p.A., Milano.

R. PETERSON, G. MOUNTFORT, P.A.D. HOLLOM, *Guida degli uccelli d'Europa.* Franco Muzzio, editore, Padova.

A. TOSCHI, *Avifauna italiana.* Editoriale Olimpia, Firenze.

BIBLIOGRAFÍA

B. BRUUN, A. SINGER, *Guía de las Aves de España y de Europa.* Ediciones Omega, S.A., Barcelona.

H. HEINZEL, R. FITTER, J. PARSLOW, *Aves de España y de Europa, Norte de África y Próximo Oriente.* Ediciones Omega, S.A., Barcelona.

S. KEITH, J. GOODERS, *Guía de las Aves de España y de Europa.* Ediciones Omega, S.A., Barcelona.

R. PETERSON, G. MOUNTFORT, P.A.D. HOLLOM, *Guía de Campo de las Aves de España y de Europa.* Ediciones Omega, S.A., Barcelona.

INDEX

SCIENTIFIC NAMES – NOMS SCIENTIFIQUES
WISSENSCHAFTLICHE NAMEN – NOMI SCIENTIFICI – NOMBRES CIENTÍFICOS

INDEX

INDEX

REGISTER

INDICE

ÍNDICE